Once upon a time

there were two brothers named Wilhelm and Jacob Grimm. They were learned scholars who filled huge libraries with dusty books for other scholars to read. Secretly however, they wrote fairy stories, the most beautiful, imaginative tales anyone ever enjoyed. By now their learned tomes have been forgotten, but the fairy stories they collected have made them immortal. This is the story of Wilhelm and Jacob, of their fantastic lives, their adventures, their romances and the fabulous tales they told. It is a story for everyone – and a happy story. For in the wonderful world of the Brothers Grimm, everyone lives happily ever after.

JOSEPH R. VOGEL   NICOLAS REISINI

In our considered opinion, Metro-Goldwyn-Mayer and Cinerama have fashioned a truly great and memorable entertainment and, in doing so, indeed, have made motion picture history.

As it should be, you and the motion picture audiences of the world are the most competent to judge those contributions to your personal entertainment pleasure.

We are confident you, and all who see The Wonderful World of the Brothers Grimm, will agree with us that magnificent dimensions never before attained have been added to the screen.

For Metro-Goldwyn-Mayer and Cinerama, our deepest appreciation.

Jo. R. Vogel

President
Metro-Goldwyn-Mayer Inc.

Nicolas Reisini

President and Chairman of the Board,
Cinerama, Inc.

 modern entertainment miracle in seven-league boots took another giant step forward on December 14, 1959 when Joseph R. Vogel, President of Metro-Goldwyn-Mayer, and Nicolas Reisini, President of Cinerama, Inc., joined to announce an agreement bringing together the unmatched creative manpower and facilities of the world's largest motion picture studios and the acclaimed Cinerama process, an exciting entertainment project.

Not a moment was lost moving Cinerama to Hollywood. Within weeks fleets of trucks were enroute from Cinerama's former headquarters at Oyster Bay, New York, to the Forum Theatre in Los Angeles. The shipments involved more than $3,000,000 in Cinerama cameras and special equipment. The Forum was redesigned and equipped as a research center aimed at the perfection of proved Cinerama techniques and the development of new ones.

The technical staffs of Metro-Goldwyn-Mayer and Cinerama immediately began an enthusiastic collaboration and round-the-clock experimentation, which produced innumerable fruitful results. Working together as a closely knit scientific team, they made many breakthroughs—visual and auditory.

The life story of the Brothers Grimm was one of the properties under consideration for the first production. Their loves, their trials, adventures and their stories—plus the opportunity of filming in the actual locale where they lived, the castled valleys of Bavaria with their rivers, mountains and forests—were carefully studied.

The decision was made.

"The Wonderful World of the Brothers Grimm" was to be the first dramatic, story-telling motion picture to be filmed in the breath-taking realism of the Cinerama process for audiences everywhere.

For many generations the folk tales and fairy stories of Wilhelm and Jacob Grimm have been a wonderful part of the world of children. Today they are as appealing as when they were written, 150 years ago, and through them fathers and mothers, grandfathers and grandmothers recapture their youth by the retelling of these timeless works.

The world of the Brothers Grimm is a rich world, a world of fantastic imaginings, where dragons prowl and witches dwell—peopled by honest woodcutters and beautiful princesses—inhabited by wicked wolves and kindly giants, where scullery maids wear glass slippers and are beloved by handsome princes.

Among the citizens of this wonderful world are characters every child has loved. And, no doubt, in the mind of every adult is the memory of a wild and wonderful tale, first told, perhaps in a cave during the dawn of time, retold through the ages and finally set down, in permanent print, in the wonderful words of the Brothers Grimm.

The stories of the Brothers Grimm are surely literature, and literature that has withstood the test of time. Their wide appeal circles the globe and illuminates childhood's wonderful world of imagination for people of all ages and all lands.

This rich, fantasy land of the Grimms, therefore, offered the perfect subject for a motion picture. But what motion picture technique could do justice to such a world of fact and fancy?

Indeed, the only answer was—CINERAMA.

The result has been an adventure in the making of motion pictures, the first Metro-Goldwyn-Mayer and Cinerama production...George Pal's "The Wonderful World of the Brothers Grimm."

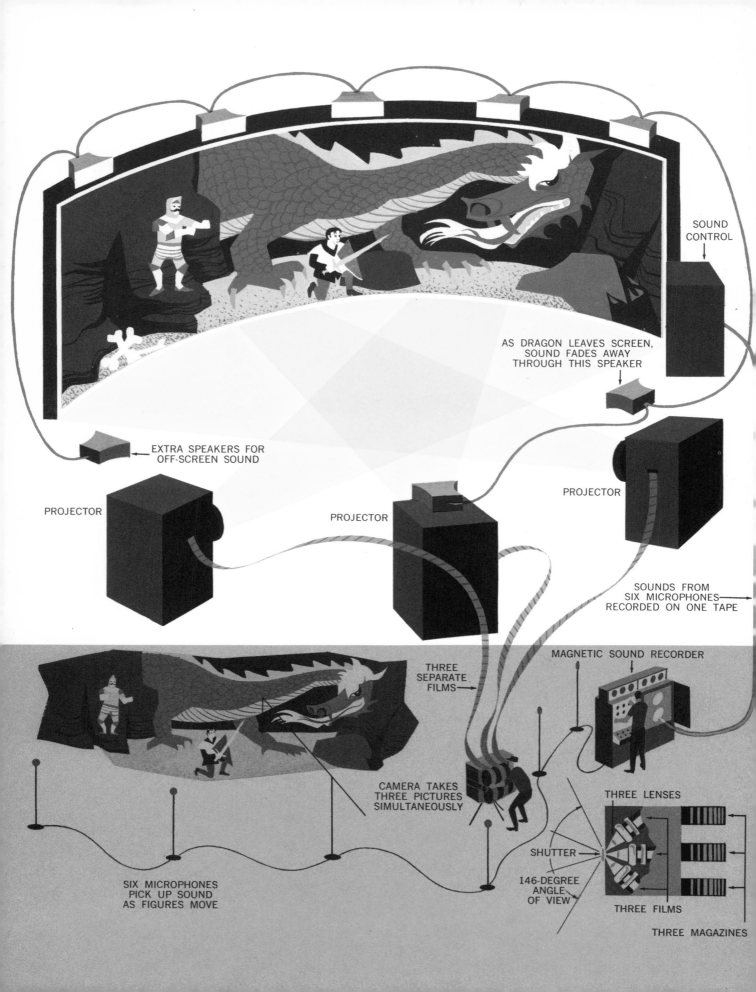

SOUND CONTROL

AS DRAGON LEAVES SCREEN, SOUND FADES AWAY THROUGH THIS SPEAKER

EXTRA SPEAKERS FOR OFF-SCREEN SOUND

PROJECTOR

PROJECTOR

PROJECTOR

SOUNDS FROM SIX MICROPHONES RECORDED ON ONE TAPE

THREE SEPARATE FILMS

MAGNETIC SOUND RECORDER

CAMERA TAKES THREE PICTURES SIMULTANEOUSLY

THREE LENSES

SHUTTER

146-DEGREE ANGLE OF VIEW

THREE FILMS

SIX MICROPHONES PICK UP SOUND AS FIGURES MOVE

THREE MAGAZINES

"The Wonderful World of the Brothers Grimm" appropriately marks an important anniversary and Cinerama's most significant milestone since the historic evening of September 30, 1952, when a privileged audience of 1100 in a New York theatre came to be shown, and remained to cheer "This is Cinerama."

In the years since Cinerama's memorable public debut, millions have thrilled to an experience of sight and sound unlike any other. The realism of the breathtakingly wide, curved Cinerama screen and seven-track sound of unsurpassed fidelity combined to wrap the world with its myriad voices around their theatre seats.

Audiences no longer were mere spectators. They toured the globe at the flicker of a Cinerama camera shutter, participants in whatever strange and exotic scene and experience Cinerama chose to poke its triple-lens, all-seeing camera—from the snow-capped Himalayas to the sun-drenched, multi-hued palette of Polynesia.

Cinerama is a tribute and monument to the faith and endless patience of the late Fred Waller, a motion picture special effects expert, and an inventive genius. The scientist in Waller was intrigued during the mid-30's by the enhanced illusion of reality created by wide-angle photography.

Waller found the answer in the human eye . . . and set out to prove that peripheral vision—what is "seen" out of the corners of our eyes—produces the sense of depth without which the world would look strange indeed.

WHAT IS CINERAMA?

Fifteen years of research and continuous experimentation finally produced the result Waller had been seeking, three cameras mounted as one, with a single shutter. The three 27 mm. lenses covered a field 146 degrees wide, approximately that of the human eye. This was the ideal range for practical and comfortable viewing in a theater.

All Cinerama lacked was a sound system to match its visual realism. Cinerama Sound was developed by the Hazard Reeves Laboratories. The matchless seven-track, seven-channel system made it possible not only to follow the action with the eyes, but with the ears as well.

With "The Wonderful World of the Brothers Grimm," Cinerama audiences see and hear more than ever before. Where the original Cinerama audience was overwhelmed by a 1700-square foot screen of ingenious louvered design, the largest ever created up to that time, the minimum Cinerama screen now installed is 3000-square feet.

The seven-channel Cinerama Sound has also undergone improvements, and now is transistorized for even more flawless tonal qualities. Further refinements have been made in the realms of projection and printing.

It can be said, in simple truth, that Cinerama is tomorrow's entertainment here to be enjoyed today.

One of the finest casts ever assembled for a motion picture appears in the magical world of the Brothers Grimm.

LAURENCE HARVEY portrays Wilhelm Grimm, who carries his head in the clouds and writes with a pen dipped in rainbow-ink. Harvey, one of the "most in demand" stars in Hollywood, came to this assignment following an imposing list of stellar performances, among them "Room at the Top," "Butterfield 8," "Walk on the Wild Side" and "Summer and Smoke."

KARL BOEHM, eminent Austrian actor, is the practical Jacob who risks everything in which he believes to help his brother. Boehm's first American role was that of the fiery Nazi sympathizer in "The Four Horsemen of the Apocalypse."

CLAIRE BLOOM, internationally famous star on both stage and screen, is Dorothea, patient, loving and the mother of three—a boy, a girl and her dreamer-husband, Wilhelm. Miss Bloom flew to Hollywood for the role directly from appearances in the London stage hit, "Altoona."

BARBARA EDEN is Greta Heinrich, the charming visitor from Berlin who manages, temporarily at least, to turn Jacob's mind from work to romance. Miss Eden was originally discovered for films in the TV show, "How to Marry a Millionaire" and recently appeared in the motion picture, "Voyage to the Bottom of the Sea."

WALTER SLEZAK, OSCAR HOMOLKA, MARTITA HUNT, IAN WOLFE, and two child stars, TAMMY MARIHUGH and BRYAN RUSSELL, round out the stellar biographical cast.

Similarly star-studded are the fairy tales.

YVETTE MIMIEUX is the beautiful "The Dancing Princess" who nightly sneaks from the palace to wear out her slippers dancing at a gypsy camp. Yvette, one of Hollywood's brightest new personalities, won acclaim for her work in "The Four Horsemen of the Apocalypse" and the delightful, "Light in the Piazza."

RUSS TAMBLYN portrays the dashing young Woodsman who steals her heart—and her secret. Tamblyn also stars in another Metro-Goldwyn-Mayer-Cinerama production, "How the West Was Won."

THE STARS

THE COBBLER'S ELVES

George Pal's Puppetoons are the "do-gooders" who help the kindly Cobbler.

BARBARA EDEN

A new girl in town — and a beautiful on but Jacob is too busy writing books.

LAURENCE HARVEY

Wilhelm Grimm, the dreamer, who believed fiction more beautiful — and more fun — than facts.

CLAIRE BLOOM

Wilhelm's wife. Lovely, gentle and very busy raising two children — and a husband.

WALTER SLEZAK

His bookstore is a haven for the Grimm brothers. His friendly wisdom is their powerful ally.

KARL BOEHM

Jacob Grimm, the scholar, who felt that legends were neither practical—nor profitable.

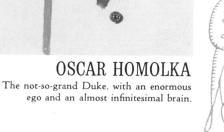

OSCAR HOMOLKA

The not-so-grand Duke. with an enormous ego and an almost infinitesimal brain.

Drawings of "The Wonderful World of the Brothers Grimm." Cast of Characters are the work of Joseph J. Smith, native Philadelphian and graduate of the Pennsylvania School of Industrial Art. Mr. Smith has become one of the most famous artists in Hollywood.

RUSS TAMBLYN

Who gambled his love against the headsman's ax and won a princess for a bride.

JIM BACKUS

The crazy mixed-up king, whose daughter needs 365 new pairs of shoes each ye

BEULAH BONDI

The lonely old gypsy who knew the secret to the fabulous cloak of invisibility.

TERRY-THOMAS

A knight-arrogant in rusty armor, with a chicken rampant on his coat-of-arms.

YVETTE MIMIEUX

The Dancing Princess, who lost her pride, her heart, but found True Love

JIM BACKUS plays the blustering King who offers the hand of the Princess and half his kingdom to anyone who discovers the secret of the worn-out slippers...and BEULAH BONDI is the hermit gypsy who befriends Tamblyn in his quest.

LAURENCE HARVEY is transformed into the kindly Cobbler as he tells the tale of "The Cobbler and the Elves" to a group of children. And along with Harvey are five of George Pal's famous PUPPETOONS who sing, dance and, incidentally, cobble shoes.

TERRY-THOMAS, British star, bows on the Cinerama screen as the boastful, dragon-hunting Knight Ludwig in the story of "The Singing Bone." The popular comedian, who has appeared in numerous British films, recently appeared in the Hollywood-made production, "Bachelor Flat."

BUDDY HACKETT, popular nightclub and TV entertainer, is Hans, Ludwig's faithful servant. Hackett has guest-starred on every leading TV show and his recent film assignments list such productions as "Everything's Ducky" and "The Music Man."

OTTO KRUGER, veteran of stage and screen, plays the King and young TV star ROBERT CRAWFORD the shepherd boy who listen to the tale of "The Singing Bone."

ARNOLD STANG is Rumpelstiltskin, the little gnome who spins straw into gold, and spokesman for the fairy tale folk who visit the bedside of Wilhelm Grimm. Stang has the distinction of being one of the few actors to achieve stardom in four different fields of entertainment, films, television, the Broadway stage and as a recording personality.

BUDDY HACKETT

Who fearlessly faced the ferociously fanged fire breathing fiend of a dragon.

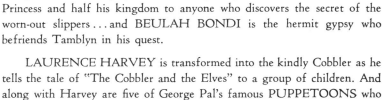

THE FAIRY TALE CHARACTERS

From fairy tale land come some famous and recognizable personalities.

THE STORY

 Once upon a time In the ornate library of the Duke, Wilhelm and Jacob Grimm are busily writing the Duke's family history, which the distinguished gentleman plans to present to the Emperor of Prussia.

Jacob, the elder, is content in the knowledge that this endeavor will buy bread for himself and Wilhelm, as well as for Wilhelm's wife and two small children.

But Wilhelm, the younger, an incurable dreamer, allows his thoughts to wander to fantastic lands peopled by giants and elves, fairies and dragons, knights and princesses.

When their employment by the Duke is threatened because of Wilhelm's fancies, Jacob insists that his brother restrict his thoughts to the job at hand. Wilhelm promises—but when a flower-vendor offers him a new story in return for the purchase of a bouquet, he succumbs. Back at home that evening he sneaks upstairs at bedtime to relate his new-found treasure to his small son and daughter who are captivated with the story of "The Dancing Princess."

Convinced that a book of fairy tales will sell, Wilhelm attempts to prove his point to the local book dealer, Stossel. He commandeers a group of children from the street to listen to another of his stories, "The Cobbler and the Elves." But Stossel is unimpressed, insisting that if Wilhelm must write fiction he write about girls.

Sent to Rhinesburg by the Duke to research the Rhinesburg branch of his family, Wilhelm heads for the cathedral to interview the priest, while Jacob goes to the Town Hall for material kept in the archives. A meeting time for the journey homeward down the Rhine is agreed upon, but Wilhelm forgets. Instead he

In her forest hut, Anna Richter fascinates village children with tales of enchanted lands.

Once again the tired earth shook to the sounds of war.

The Brothers Grimm sail on the oldest side-wheeler in Germany.
Wilhelm discovers brother Jacob has fallen in love.

follows a group of children to the hut of a story-teller in the Black Forest—and listens outside while she tells her young friends the exciting story of "The Singing Bone."

Hurrying back to meet Jacob, Wilhelm slips while crossing a stream. His wooden writing case breaks open and he is unaware of the fact that the Duke's precious manuscript is floating out to the sea.

Furious at this turn of events, Jacob determines to dissolve the writing partnership with his brother, move out of the family home and marry his sweetheart, the beautiful Greta Heinrich.

But Wilhelm is taken seriously ill. Unconscious, in his bed, Wilhelm dreams a strange dream. All of the fairy tale folk of his imagination are lifted through his second-story window by a huge giant. They beg him not to die—for if he dies they will never be born as he, alone, can write their stories. They further entreat him to at least give them names. Wilhelm agrees. He names them Snow White—and her Seven Dwarfs, Little Red Riding Hood, Hansel and Gretel, Cinderella, the Frog Prince, the Queen Bee—and last, but not least, Rumpelstiltskin.

Wilhelm recovers, but his brush with death causes a change of heart in Jacob, who agrees to keep the partnership. Both of them will write fairy tales as well as more serious volumes.

The brothers plunge into their work, and gradually their fame spreads. While Jacob's books are accepted by schools and colleges, families gather around in the evenings to hear fathers and mothers read the fairy tales of Wilhelm.

* * *

One afternoon the Grimms are visited by a noteworthy delegation headed by their former employer, the Duke, and their good friend Stossel. Through them the brothers learn they have been appointed to the Berlin Academy. This not only means they will be given time and money to continue their work . . . but a home in Berlin as well.

On the train for Berlin, Wilhelm turns to Jacob.

"You were right all along," he says, "the Academy didn't even mention the fairy tales, only the other books . . ."

"What we did, we did together," answers Jacob.

Wilhelm is disappointed, for the honor is really his brother's. The train pulls into the station. There to meet them is a top-hatted delegation from the Berlin Academy. Jacob steps forward to deliver his prepared speech when suddenly his voice is drowned in an uproar. Children appear from everywhere, children shouting . . .

"Tell us a story, Mr. Grimm . . . please tell us a story."

Jacob pushes Wilhelm forward. Almost choking with emotion, Wilhelm begins . . .

"Once upon a time," he says, "there were two brothers . . ."

And as his voice dies away over the screen rise the words . . . "And they lived happily ever after."

It's a festive day in the royal palace, and the lovers live happily ever after.

THE DANCING PRINCESS

The beautiful Princess runs down the stairs to her waiting coach.

A Princess plots the downfall of a Woodsman who risks his head to find her secret.

In the magic firelight of a gypsy camp the Princess dances with a handsome, masked stranger.

THE SINGING BONE

Brave Hans challenges the dragon while cowardly Ludwig shouts instructions.

Hans rides high on the back of the dragon.

Sir Ludwig and his servant Hans are draggin' their feet looking for the dragon.

A quaking Sir Ludwig listens while the singing bone tells of his cowardice.

THE COBBLER AND THE ELVES

The Ballerina must have slippers for the King's Christmas party.

Christmas morning the Cobbler
carries his Elves to the orphanage.

Wilhelm and Jacob are appointed to the Berlin Royal Academy.

Toward Berlin and fame ride Wilhelm, Jacob and Wilhelm's family.
The Duke strikes a noble attitude as he poses for his portrait.

THE BACKGROUND STORY

The fascinating saga of Wilhelm and Jacob Grimm had its beginning "once upon a time" in the little town of Cegled, Hungary, where a small boy pored over a large book. The boy was George Pal; the book Grimms' Fairy Tales.

"The story has always spurred my imagination," Pal, the producer of "The Wonderful World of the Brothers Grimm" recalls. "The characters became my intimate friends and we never outgrew each other."

In this respect, George Pal shares a thrill of fantasy with people all over the world.

For 150 years the compilation of fairy tales by the Brothers Grimm have been best-selling literary works the world over.

Their stories have been printed in 210 editions and 30 different languages in the past six years alone.

The earliest edition collected by the Grimm Museum in Kassel, Germany, is dated 1812. The most recent, 1960.

Italy leads all countries with 30 translations of the works, closely followed by versions in English, French, Spanish, Dutch and Russian.

There is not a language existent in the world today in which the stories of Wilhelm and Jacob Grimm have not been published.

Children crowd the station to hear Wilhelm's famous words "Once upon a time."

The fairy tale folk visit Wilhelm and Dorothea who shares his dream.

It was 16 years after George Pal arrived in Hollywood that he had a chance to make his dream of bringing these stories to the screen come true. At this time, through his first association with Metro-Goldwyn-Mayer, he made the delightful and successful "tom thumb."

Seven years later Pal stumbled onto a volume written by Dr. Hermann Gerstner and titled, "The Grimm Brothers."

Here, in this book of letters, was his long-sought insight into the personal lives of the two authors. Pieced together they supplied a fascinating documentary story — their loves, their romances, their friends, their neighbors, their struggles, failures and successes.

"This became the nucleus of our story," Pal said. "For seven years we worked to complete the script. But never during this time did I dare to dream that our story would reach the screen in Cinerama."

The script was completed simultaneously with an agreement between Cinerama and Metro-Goldwyn-Mayer to produce story-telling films in the fabulous medium.

Both MGM and Cinerama executives were quick to recognize the wide, family appeal of the story and its effective adaptability to the new process.

While production wheels and all of the vast resources of a great studio swung into action, Producer-Director George Pal and Henry Levin, selected to direct the biographical script, flew overseas to scout locations.

Oddly enough, the story offered sections of the world never before covered by the globe-trotting Cinerama cameras... namely Bavaria and the Rhine River Valley country.

Wilhelm and Jacob arrive at Rhineburg as the townsfolk prepare for their colorful Wine Festival.

A fairy tale castle high in the Bavarian Alps.

Historic Weikersheim Castle is the background for colorful action.

The first stop for Pal, Levin and the crew was, naturally enough, Kassel, the actual birthplace of the famous brothers. But the quaint and medieval town of Kassel they had expected to find had been totally destroyed during the war and in its place stood a modern city of glass and steel.

Pal and Levin sought a town from the past; a town seemingly untouched by modern development and progress; a town with cobbled streets, slant-roof buildings, a town square—something straight from the story books.

They found it. It was Rothenburg ob der Tauber, a tiny Medieval Franconian city.

During the latter days of World War II it, also, had been scarred by bombs. But the city fathers, fully-realizing its picturesque allure to tourists, hired an architect-artist to restore it to its original state.

It was in Rothenburg that much of the biographical story was filmed. Near the town, famous castles such as Weikersheim and Neuschwanstein were made available. Permission was granted to film inside as well as outside the castle walls, the first time such a concession was made to a film company.

Regensburg proved another spot of photogenic interest. Here was the Regensburg Cathedral, the exact type of rococco architecture they sought. Here, too, Pal and Levin discovered the world famed Regensburg Boys Choir which they persuaded to sing for a sequence in the production.

The lush, Rhine River Valley from the deck of a paddlewheeler; the romantic Lorelei Rock; the quaint village of Dinkelsbuehl; the Bavarian countryside touched with the brilliant, flaming color of fall; the Black Forest where tiny, good luck Elves hide in the leaves of the trees; the great castle at Neuschwanstein; the cobbled streets and turreted walls of Rothenburg; the quaint shops and colorful street vendors.

Here is, indeed, "The Wonderful World of the Brothers Grimm" as they saw it — and as you will live it.

Today the fantasy and beauty of their fairy tales, augmented by the emotion-packed lives of the authors, have been touched by 20th century magic.

What a pity it is that the visionary and talented Wilhelm and Jacob could not have lived to see the sorcery of their words and their deeds come to life in Cinerama.

 Once **upon a time** Metro-Goldwyn-Mayer-Cinerama went from the heights to the depths in securing office space in the tiny German town of Rothenburg. Business offices were located in the tower of the City Hall. Located high above the street it was reached only by means of a steep, circular staircase.

The temporary film laboratory was at the building's other extreme, in the City Hall's dungeon. Portions of this underground cavern were used as the local jail. As a result a duplicate key for the company had to be made — the first duplicate key struck off in more than 400 years.

* * *

Never in the history of films has a single camera had more adventures than the Cinerama unit assigned to the production. It was mounted inside a "drum" and rolled down a hill to simulate the gyrating universe as seen through the eyes of Russ Tamblyn.

It was mounted on a sled to absorb the shock of the cobbled streets.

It was strapped upside down beneath a coach where it caught the thundering hoofs of a team of spirited horses.

It was bolted to the helm of an ancient paddle-wheeler and dipped its eyes in the Rhine River.

It was mounted on a thirty-foot scaffolding inside the famous Regensburg Cathedral.

It was strapped to a swing where it sailed back and forth above the snapping jaws of a dragon.

It was mounted on a platform slung beneath a helicopter where it floated over the famous Rhine River Valley.

PRODUCTION NOTES

In this day of modern road surfacing, paving cobbles are hard to find. When it was necessary to tear apart one of Rothenburg's ancient cobbled streets for a scene in the film, permission was granted only if the company agreed to number each cobble as it was removed to insure its proper replacement.

* * *

The beautiful castles used in the film, some of them built by the Mad Emperor, Ludwig II, are valued at some $500,000,000.

Cameras prepare for a scene in Weikersheim gardens.

The colorful port of Oberspay becomes Rhineburg for the film

GEORGE PAL THE PRODUCER

Once In bringing "The Wonderful World of the Brothers Grimm" to the world of entertainment, **upon** Producer-director George Pal realizes a dream of long standing.
a time It is appropriate that Pal should be among the first producers chosen for this history-making assignment of combining a dramatic story with the astounding photographic process, Cinerama, because, through the years, Pal has been a motion picture revolutionary.

He was the first producer-director to combine animated puppets with real actors, a technique which he uses again in the fairy tale sequence, "The Cobbler and the Elves." The puppets, which he has named Puppetoons, are also his own invention and were responsible for winning him his first of six Academy Awards.

From childhood, Pal leaned toward the artistic, graduating from the Budapest Academy of Arts with a degree in Architecture. With building at a standstill, however, he turned toward his second love, cartooning, and was soon creating attention-getting advertisements for leading European concerns. It was his creation of an animated cigarette that eventually led to the development of the Puppetoons, and from the Puppetoons to Hollywood.

In Hollywood he became interested in a modern application of his puppet techniques, working toward combining live action with puppet animation. The first step in this direction came when he designed the animated squirrel playing opposite Jimmy Durante in "The Great Rupert."

"Destination Moon," first Technicolor picture dealing with a science fiction subject followed and since then Pal's string of box-office hits has continued unbroken with such films as "When Worlds Collide," "War of the Worlds," "The Naked Jungle," "tom thumb" and "The Time Machine."

The ancient steam-propelled side-wheeler, on which Wilhelm and Jacob travel down the Rhine, is the oldest such craft in Germany. Named the Oskar Huber it was commandeered for film service just three days before it was scheduled to retire to a spot of honor in the famous ship museum at Mainz.

* * *

Local museums, anxious to cooperate in bringing the story of two national heroes to the screen, threw open their doors to supply important properties. Among these was a cannon actually used by Napoleon during the Napoleonic Wars and fired by the troops in one of the filmed battle sequences. Street signs, vendors carts, to say nothing of priceless text books written by the Brothers Grimm were at the company's disposal.

BEHIND THE CAMERAS

"The Wonderful World of the Brothers Grimm" comes to the screen as an example of top teamwork between two leaders in the world of entertainment — Metro-Goldwyn-Mayer and Cinerama.

Three of the industry's finest writing talents collaborated on the many-faceted script.

David Harmon, with more than 150 television and motion picture credits, wrote the original draft of the Brothers Grimm.

Charles Beaumont, TV, short story and novel author, and winner of the 1961 Playboy Award for writing excellence, shares honors for the screen play along with William Roberts, author of a score of screen plays and TV productions.

Credit for the breathtaking photography goes to Cinematographer Paul Vogel. Vogel, a veteran at his art with more than 30 years behind the cameras, won an Academy Oscar for his work on the film "Battleground."

The charming and authentic sets, more than 75 at the studio alone, are the work of George B. Davis together with Edward Carfagno. Carfagno, who holds an Oscar for his art direction of "Ben-Hur," now has the distinction, along with Davis, of being the first to design sets expressly for the Cinerama cameras.

Literally thousands of sketches went into the creation of the wardrobe. These were the works of Mary Wills, artist and designer who ran the gamut from homespuns to 14 karat gold cloth for the assignment. During her career as a designer of film wardrobes, Miss Wills has garnered five Academy nominations.

Heading the Cinerama staff on the film as Production Supervisor was Coleman T. Conroy, Jr.

Conroy has been closely associated with Cinerama since 1952 following a career as an instructor of cinematography in Texas and Louisiana, and a period in the professional camera department of Bell and Howell. With Cinerama he became photographic director of the Cinerama camera department, guiding the construction and conducting tests for the first three Cinerama cameras.

Conroy's crew was made up of Pete Gibbons, camera engineer, who devised the animation camera especially for sequences in "Wonderful World"; camera engineer, Erik Rondum; CinemaSound expert Fred Bosch; and Ray Sharplis, who designed, among other things, the intricate platform that housed the Cinerama camera beneath a helicopter.

This group of experts, together with Metro-Goldwyn-Mayer technicians, completed the breakthrough into the Cinerama, story-telling medium.

Beautiful Neuschwanstein Castle houses the royal family of "The Dancing Princess" fairy tale.

HENRY LEVIN, who directed the biographical script for "The Wonderful World of the Brothers Grimm," was born in Trenton, New Jersey and had early exposure to the entertainment business through a theatrical boarding house owned by his parents.

This well established interest declared itself later when, after graduating from the University of Pennsylvania with a B.S. Degree in Economics, he left his first job as a Wall Street bond trader to work with a stock company in East Hampton, Long Island.

His love of the drama saw him as an assistant stage manager for the New York Theater Guild, stage manager for Brock Pemberton and as operator of a summer theater in Bass Rocks, Massachusetts with Martin Manulis as his partner. Whenever backstage duties permitted, Levin would appear as a performer in the various productions.

In 1949, prompted by a growing interest in films, Levin travelled to the West Coast. His first Hollywood position was as a dialogue coach at Columbia. Sixteen months later he was made a director.

Levin's long list of hits include such motion pictures as "Bernardine," "April Love," "The Remarkable Mr. Penny-packer," "Journey to the Center of the Earth," "Adventures of Aladdin" and the record-breaking "Where the Boys Are."

THE DIRECTOR

One of the scenic views of the Grimms' Rhine Journey.

THE MUSIC

Two of the brightest names in the world of music share honors in "The Wonderful World of the Brothers Grimm"—Bob Merrill for his themes and songs—both words and music—and Leigh Harline for the music score.

Merrill, whose "Carnival" is a recent Broadway hit, began a show business career while still in his teens and today holds the astounding record of having more than 20 tunes on the national "hit parade." In addition to "Carnival" he has written music for two other Broadway attention-getters—"New Girl in Town" and "Take Me Along."

It was in 1950 that Merrill first startled the music world with his song, "If I Knew You Were Comin' I'd Have Baked a Cake." This he followed with a parade of other popular favorites among them "How Much Is That Doggie in the Window," "Sparrow in the Tree-top," and "My Truly, Truly Fair," to mention but a few.

For "The Wonderful World of the Brothers Grimm" Merrill penned words and music for the four songs, "Ah-oom," "Christmas Land," the humorous "Dee-Are-A-Gee-O-En" (Dragon) and "The Dancing Princess." His themes are "Gypsy Fire," "Above the Stars," and "The Wonderful World of the Brothers Grimm." The music for "The Singing Bone" was written by Bob Merrill with words by Charles Beaumont.

Leigh Harline, another musician well known to Hollywood, adds a new highlight to his brilliant career with his music score. A double Academy Award winner in 1940 for his song "When You Wish Upon a Star" and his score for "Pinocchio," Harline has such top musical credits as "Snow White and the Seven Dwarfs," "Pride of the Yankees," "The Bachelor and the Bobby Soxer," "Miracle of the Bells," "Broken Lance," "Susan Slept Here," "Facts of Life," "The Honeymoon Machine" and many more.

Appearing with the Metro-Goldwyn-Mayer Symphony Orchestra is Ruth Welcome, zither stylist and Capitol Recording star. Miss Welcome, the only woman in America to play the zither professionally, learned the instrument as a child in Freiburg in the Black Forest country of Germany and in Basle, Switzerland.

Another MGM Cinerama Production

HOW THE WEST WAS WON

"HOW THE WEST WAS WON," the biggest, most exciting outdoor adventure story ever filmed, will be the next presentation of Metro-Goldwyn-Mayer and Cinerama.

Many of the greatest stars in Hollywood accepted important roles. These include Carroll Baker, Lee J. Cobb, Henry Fonda, Carolyn Jones, Karl Malden, Gregory Peck, George Peppard, Robert Preston, Debbie Reynolds, James Stewart, Eli Wallach, John Wayne and Richard Widmark. The co-stars include Brigid Bazlen, Walter Brennan, David Brian, Andy Devine, Raymond Massey, Agnes Moorehead, Henry (Harry) Morgan, Thelma Ritter, Mickey Shaughnessy and Russ Tamblyn. The narration is by Spencer Tracy.

In "How the West Was Won" you will experience through the magic of Cinerama a raft trip through swirling river rapids, the cannonading at the Battle of Shiloh, the thundering stampede of 2,000 buffalo, the breakneck chase as warring Indians pursue a wagon train and breath-taking gun battle between lawmen and outlaws aboard a speeding train.

To capture the color and size of the real West, MGM camera crews literally traveled the length and breadth of America, from the Canadian to the Mexican borders and from Kentucky to the splenderous High Sierra. Glacier-fed rivers of the Pacific Northwest, the snow-capped Rockies of Colorado, the rugged desert of Arizona and the Black Hills of South Dakota — sacred ground of the Sioux — are some of the scenic wonders that form mural-like backgrounds to the action, drama and romance of "How the West Was Won."

Three directors — Henry Hathaway, John Ford and George Marshall, representing 150 years of motion picture experience — were chosen to direct "How the West Was Won," the most physically difficult production ever brought to the screen.

Produced by Bernard Smith and written by James Webb, "How the West Was Won" is the story of America's westward expansion from the 1830's to the 1880's as experienced by three generations of a pioneer family.

"How the West Was Won" opens with the movement of settlers down the Erie Canal to the sprawling Ohio River Valley frontier, then moves in succession through the California Gold Rush, the Civil War in the West, the building of the first trans-continental railroad and, finally, the triumph of law and order over the outlawry that plagued the great Southwest.

One of the breathtaking moments from "How the West was Won."

THE BOOK

Wilhelm Grimm	Laurence Harvey
Jacob Grimm	Karl Boehm
Dorothea Grimm	Claire Bloom
Stossel	Walter Slezak
Greta Heinrich	Barbara Eden
The Duke	Oscar Homolka
Rumpelstiltskin	Arnold Stang
Story Teller	Martita Hunt
Gruber	Ian Wolfe
Miss Bettenhausen	Betty Garde
Mrs. von Dittersdorf	Cheerio Meredith
Friedrich Grimm	Bryan Russell
Pauline Grimm	Tammy Marihugh
The Priest	Walter Rilla

THE DANCING PRINCESS

The Princess	Yvette Mimieux
The Woodsman	Russ Tamblyn
The King	Jim Backus
The Gypsy	Beulah Bondi
The Prime Minister	Clinton Sundberg

THE COBBLER AND THE ELVES

The Cobbler	Laurence Harvey
The Mayor	Walter Brooke
The Ballerina	Sandra Gale Bettin
The Hunter	Robert Foulk

And the
PUPPETOONS

THE SINGING BONE

Ludwig	Terry-Thomas
Hans	Buddy Hackett
The King	Otto Kruger
The Shepherd	Robert Crawford, Jr.
The Spokesman	Sydney Smith

The Cast